KT-143-559

ONE HUNDRED WAYS
FOR
A Cat to Train Its Human

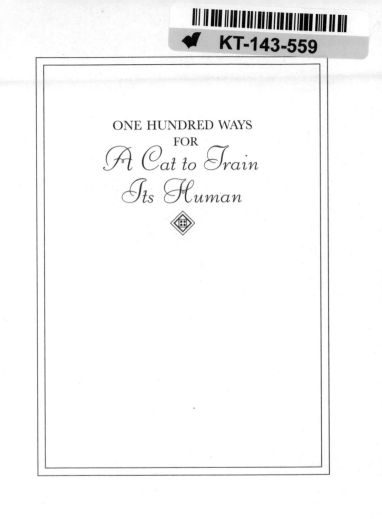

ONE HUNDRED WAYS
FOR
*A Cat to Train
Its Human*

BY

Celia Haddon

Hodder & Stoughton
LONDON SYDNEY AUCKLAND

Copyright © 2001 by Celia Haddon
in the arrangement

First published in Great Britain in 2001

The right of Celia Haddon to be identified as the
Author of the Work has been asserted by her in
accordance with the Copyright, Designs
and Patents Act 1988.

15 17 19 20 18 16 14

All rights reserved. No part of this publication
may be reproduced, stored in a retrieval system or
transmitted, in any form or by any means, without
the prior written permission of the publisher,
nor be otherwise circulated in any form of
binding or cover other than that in which
it is published and without a similar
condition being imposed on the
subsequent purchaser.

British Library Cataloguing in Publication Data
A record for this book is available from
the British Library

ISBN 0 340 78605 1

Printed and bound in Great Britain

Hodder & Stoughton
A Division of Hodder Headline Ltd
338 Euston Road
London NW1 3BH

This book is dedicated to
Freda and Daisy, whose Burmese
obedience training has made Judith
into the perfect pet.

Contents

Understanding Your Human

Dogs may have masters. We cats have staff. Keep this in mind for a happy cat-human relationship.

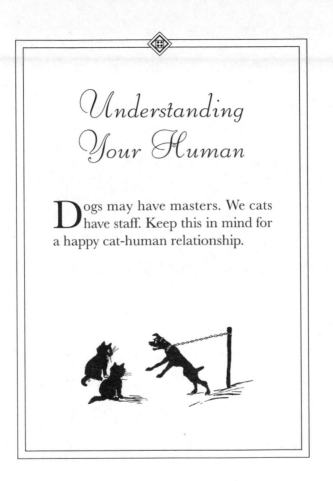

To make sure your human understands that you are alpha cat, head of the family and pack leader, institute a status-reduction programme immediately. Your human must learn that you have first right to all chairs, beds and doorways. You expect to be fed first and go through doors before it does. A happy human knows its place in the pecking order – well below that of the cat.

Remember. Humans have the mental age of a one-week-old blind kitten. They cannot express themselves in body language because they have no tail and no whiskers; their hair can't stand up and their ears are completely inflexible. They can learn only a few words from the huge body-language feline vocabulary.

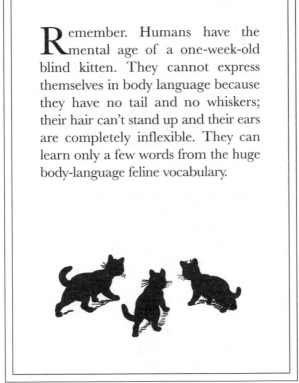

Though humans cannot speak cat, they vocalise repeatedly. Most of their vocalisations are meaningless and can be safely ignored.

A few human vocalisations are worth remembering. Keep an ear open for one aversive human vocalisation – the 'vet' noise. When you hear this, leave home for the whole day or, if you are kept indoors, hide.

You may also detect a repeated sound such as 'Sam', 'Tibbles' or 'Sooty'. This sound marks a primitive human attempt at the kitten-call chirrup. Dogs come when they are called. We cats take a message and get back later – maybe.

A series of high-pitched human shrieks can mean either delight or fear. When these noises follow the gift of a mouse on the bed, we can safely guess that the reaction is one of delight at such a delicious present.

Sounds that are worth responding to include the noise of a tin opening, the cutting noise of a knife on a board, or the rustle of a package. Position yourself fast in the kitchen.

In the course of being domesticated by cats, humans lost most of their sense of smell. The obvious scent messages of chin-rubbing and claw-scratching mean nothing to them. Your human does not realise that this is your way of making a house into a home and mixing your smell with the human smell.

If your human doesn't understand you, take up social work among lonely humans in your street. They may be at home, when your human is out at work. In winter, this means their central heating will be on, when yours is off. It's never too late to find a second home.

Obedience Training

— Rewards and Punishments

Obedience training for your human starts with rewarding it for good behaviour and punishing it for bad. As human beings want to please, rewards are simple. Punishment is a claw-and-ordure issue.

Take control of your human and never let it initiate an action. If your human walks towards you, walk away. If it tries to pet you, turn your back. All petting and games should be at your timing, not its choice.

Be unpredictable. One day be all over your human, the next day ignore it. Inconsistency trains better than reliability. Or as learning theory puts it, an intermittent reward schedule is more effective than a continuous reward schedule.

Humans love being petted. Reward them with purrs, head-butting and rubbing against their legs. Leave a love token of fur on their new clothes. After all, fur's fur. They deserve it.

Knead their lap with your front paws. Humans appreciate this kitten-like gesture but find it extremely painful. Have fun seeing their mixture of pleasure and pain.

If you are a Siamese or of oriental extraction, you will be able to train your human by using your voice in the command yowl. Most Siamese train by yowling repeatedly and rewarding their human with silence when it does the right thing.

Ignoring your human by withdrawing your attention is a powerful training tool. Simply turn your back firmly away from the erring human, giving no eye contact, and sit quietly thinking of higher things.

Excessive attention-seeking by humans – silly kitten-like calls, maladroit attempts at petting, or interference with sleep – may be quelled by a hiss. Even the most retarded human recognises that the hiss means, 'Get lost!'

Hair-balls are the best way of punishing your humans for not grooming you. Throw up where a sleepy human will have a surprise – near the bed, by the coffee machine, near the fridge or on the stairs.

Growling, backing-up with fur erect, and tail-lashing are other recognisable deterrents, which even humans can understand.

Claw and ordure are your ultimate weapons. Only in the most severe cases of human mis-behaviour should you use claw enforcement by scratching or biting. The use of ordure by spraying or pooping is the final deterrent.

Attention, Purrlease!

Place your bottom firmly on the newspaper your human is reading, being careful to cover the area scanned by its eyes.

Pause with your tail up and waving gently in front of the TV or start patting the screen with your paw. If this doesn't work, sit on the TV with your tail hanging down.

If you have a gentle and loving human, claw its tights or nip its ankles. Do not do this with aggressive humans, as it can result in the boot.

Jump on the mantelpiece or dressing-table and swipe off anything standing there. This is useful for waking up sleeping humans.

D ive-bomb your human from the bedhead or nearby furniture to wake it up. Aim at groin, breast or head.

S it in the hand basin just before your human intends to shave.

Enter the litterbox and d-i-i-ig deep, making sure you scratch the plastic of the tray so as to make an interesting squeaking noise. This works particularly well during mealtimes if the litterbox is in the kitchen. A blizzard of litter thrown out through the entrance also gets attention.

Play with the twinkly balls and silvery string placed on the Christmas tree. If you leap up to seize a decoration, the tree will crash to the floor and bring the whole household running.

Climb up a tree or a roof. Cling there, mewing. When your human tries to rescue you, climb higher. Eventually a large red engine and several beefy people in uniform will turn up. Wait until they start climbing up the ladder, then leap effortlessly down.

Chew telephone wires and electric flex. You won't have to chew very much before your human picks you up.

Walk over the computer keyboard, being careful to press down the keys. Use your body to shield the interesting additions to the screen. Stand on one key so that a character repeats itself endlessly.

Boycott the cat-flap. Sit on the window ledge until your human lets you in through the window. This is particularly good fun in a gale.

Eat a house plant. If you don't like the taste, tear it to shreds. Eat grass in the garden and come in to throw up on the best settee.

Practise projectile vomiting on the new carpet, or better still on the bed. It's a good gag to wake your human up in the middle of the night.

If all else fails, spray. Boy, does attention-seeking spraying work! A truly stupid human will try to clear up using a scented cleaning fluid. This smells like cat urine and will make the marking point even more interesting. Top it up again.

Mealtime Manners

Feeding rituals make mealtimes fun. Refuse to eat unless your human holds your tail, strokes your back, or sits beside you on the cold kitchen floor. Insist on eating only on the table, on the sofa, or even on the stairs. If you are a good trainer, you can train in a whole chain of human behaviour, such as requiring your human to lie flat on its tummy, put its head in your dish, and make a 'yum-yum' noise, before you eat.

Sit in front of the fridge and mew. Rub against your human's legs to train it to give you food on command. If necessary, discipline it by nipping its ankle or clawing its tights.

Do not *ever* in any circumstances eat food that has been left down longer than ten minutes.

Lick up the jelly and the gravy and leave the rest.

Refuse to eat from a can of food that has been opened for a previous meal. This will help train your owner into buying a new small can for each meal, and we cats know that this is the most expensive and tasty sort of food.

Never eat offerings straight from the fridge. The correct temperature for all food is lukewarm, the temperature of a freshly killed mouse.

Humans go hunting in super-markets and bring back food for you. It is your job to train them into bringing home the right brand by positive reinforcement. Purr intensely while eating expensive food and refuse to eat the cheap kind.

After refusing to eat the inferior cat food, eat a small piece of dry bread from the floor or table. This will purrsuade your owner that you are starving and a new, more expensive can must immediately be opened.

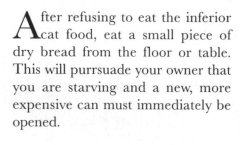

Cheap food should be treated with the Litter Technique. Circle the bowl and attempt to cover its contents with imaginary litter. This shows what you think it is.

Encourage your human to share its meals. Sit on the table very close to its plate and watch each mouthful. Intercept food between plate and human mouth with a paw.

Raid the dustbin or the kitchen trashcan. Pull out a piece of chicken skin and drag it round the room. Leave it half-eaten near the fridge.

Eat a spider out of the bath. You
will find this has an unexpected
effect on your human and may well
be greeted with a shriek – or laughter.
For full effect, eat the spider after you
have refused a meal.

Dine out. In urban areas there are plenty of cat-flaps allowing access to another cat's dinner.

Two-time your human with another human feeder. A regular social round can be set up so that you enjoy two breakfasts and several lunches before coming home for dinner with your regular human partner.

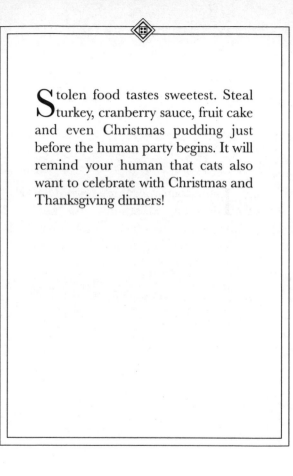

Stolen food tastes sweetest. Steal turkey, cranberry sauce, fruit cake and even Christmas pudding just before the human party begins. It will remind your human that cats also want to celebrate with Christmas and Thanksgiving dinners!

House-Training Your Human

House-train your human from the day you walk into your new home. Given encouragement, humans are clean creatures, but they need to be taught the elements of purrsonal hygiene for cats – proper litterbox cleaning routines, feline litter preferences and litterbox location.

Your human has changed the nice expensive litter to a horrid cheap one, made of rocks or, worse still, wooden blocks. Either dig most of this out of the tray or, if it is just too heavy to shift, do not dig at all. Just leave a stinky calling card on the top of the litter, uncovered.

If the message doesn't get through, leave the same calling card just outside the litterbox.

If your human is not clearing up the litterbox often enough, wait till it has cleaned it out, then nip in and perform immediately. This will show that you like a clean tray, not a dirty one.

If your human has made the litter smell wrong by adding a scented deodorant, boycott the litterbox. Go outside the box or elsewhere.

Liners can get in the way of a good dig. Dig up the liner and see if you can pull it halfway out of the litter tray. Sure, it's messy, but it makes the point.

Has your human changed the site of the litterbox? Naturally, you want it back in its old and rightful place? Simply use the old area – too bad that the tray is no longer there. Or go in the sink.

If the soil in the flower-bed has been dug over in the garden, your human has made you a nice new latrine. Use it.

Other human-made latrines include large pots with house plants and soil around them, window boxes, seed trays in the potting shed, or almost anywhere in the greenhouse. Keep an eye out for heaps of builders' sand, open bags of peat, children's sandpits or gravelled areas with small gravel. These make nice places to go too. Try leaving your calling card on the lawn.

Prized plants in the rock garden are excellent for marking your territory. Back up against the miniature conifers and let fly.

Other good places to spray include just outside the back door (so your human can get a good whiff), and on garden instruments left lying about, plant labels, garden chairs and tables the night before a garden party.

Claiming Your Purrsonal Space

Don't be selfish. Allow your human to use the armchairs when you are out hunting or busy elsewhere in the house. Just make sure it gets off when *you* want to sit there.

To get a male human off an armchair, jump onto the back of it, hold down his head with a firm paw and lick his bald patch. Control is a c-attitude of mind.

If the door is shut, scratch the carpet outside to shreds. Doors should remain half open at all times, especially doors leading to the garden during a snowstorm. Humans should be feline automatic doors.

S ome cats feel it is bad for discipline to let humans up on the bed. But be generous and share. They do so love sleeping next to you.

L etting humans sleep inside the bed with you is also good way to ensure a night-long hot-water bottle.

Reclaim the duvet during the night. This is done by gentle but firm pressure, inching your way so that the sleeping human cannot help but move off your space.

Anything soft – clean laundry, mink coats, lingerie, ball-gowns – makes a cat bed, except a newly purrchased cat bed.

To mark your territory, scratch wherever it feels good – chairs, table legs, carpets, mats, wallpaper (especially if it has stripes), doors and beds. Scratching makes a house into a home. Everything makes a good scratching post except a scratching post.

If your territory is threatened by a new cat, a new human, a dog or the feline bully next door, spray. Well-trained humans will realise this is a cry for help and call in a cat behaviour counsellor to help them understand your psychological need for safe territory.

If this cry for help goes un-recognised, mix your scent with your human's intimate scent, by pooping on the bed. This will encourage mean humans to pay up for the cat behaviour counsellor – fast.

If humans react with rage instead of counselling, don't be a victim of domestic violence. Battered cats can usually find a refuge somewhere up the street. Rehome yourself.

Fur Play for Felines

Anything not nailed down is a cat toy, except a new cat toy.

Humans often bring home unwanted gifts like brightly coloured little balls, fake fur oblongs roughly in the shape of a mouse, or horrid little gadgets smelling of artificial catnip. Ignore these. Why can't they bring home a real mouse?

Train your human to play cat and mouse with you. At first, when you pounce on it, it may flinch. But they will soon learn there is no cat game without pain.

Get plenty of sleep during the day so that you can have fun with your human in the early hours of the morning.

Dressing-gown cords are fun. If you pull hard at the cord, the dressing-gown will come off the hook in the middle of the night.

Play with the laces on human shoes. This is most fun in the morning when humans are in a hurry to leave the house.

Lure your human into petting you. Then, when it is happily involved, bite the hand that pets you. Use your two back legs for an exquisitely painful scratch. This is the petting and biting game.

An aquarium of goldfish or tropical fish is interactive feline TV. And when you are bored, they make a good TV dinner.

Do some catnip. Lie flat on your back and roll your eyeballs. Making your human laugh is the key to a continuous supply. A laughing human soon becomes a catnip drug dealer.

Real mice make for the best games of all. Bring them into the house and let them go under the bed. Then you can play with them later, during the night.

Store your mice (dead or alive) under the fridge, inside a shoe, tucked away in a handbag or even in the toaster. This way, they are safe from interfering humans until you need them.

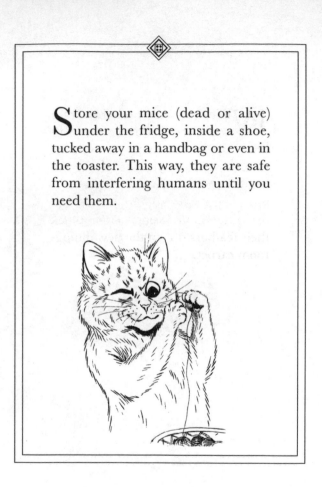

While you can probably train your human to allow you to bring in mice, it is almost impossible to train it not to interfere when you bring in birds. So make sure your birds are already dead before bringing them inside. Then pluck their feathers off on the new dining-room carpet.

For the ambitious cat, there may be big game in the next-door garden, only partly protected by wire netting. Your human will make a delighted shriek if you bring home a rabbit or a guinea-pig.

If prey is scarce in your neighbourhood, consider bringing in smaller creatures like worms (pleasantly wriggly), beetles (crisp and crunchy) or even butterflies and moths (fun and fluttery).

In urban areas be imaginative in your hunting. Bring home new prey like mink stoles, teddy bears, old underwear, or hot sausages from a summer barbecue. For some reason humans find this kind of cat burglary very funny.

Purrsonal Problems

If you hear the word 'flea', flee! If you are not fast enough on your feet, they will spray you, put smelly collars on you or pour stinky liquid on the back of your neck.

Some humans are in denial about fleas. When you get really itchy, don't just scratch. Start pulling your fur out as a protest. (OK, so you don't like flea treatments either, but that's their problem, not yours.)

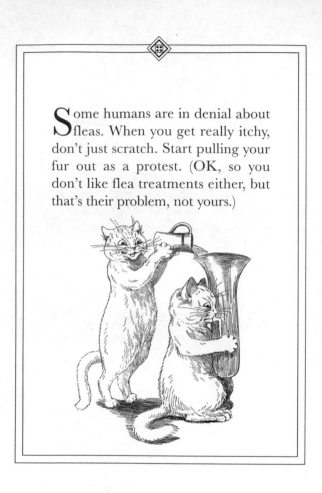

When a human pokes a pill into your mouth, do not spit it out immediately. Put it into the side of your mouth and go away into another room. Retreat under the bed and spit it out. Most humans are not clever enough to realise what you have done.

Other ways of avoiding swallowing a pill include: running up the curtains and drapes, jumping on to the top of the wardrobe, climbing up a tree, hiding on the roof, crawling up the chimney, diving out of the window, sitting very quietly indeed in a dark cupboard.

Dogs need to understand that you are Top Cat and pack leader with nine lives to their one. Steal their food. Sleep in their beds. Sneer at them from a great height. Keep them alert for your sudden attack. Bar access to your human at all times. Cats rule, OK!

Dogs provide running practice for cats, but you can use an element of surprise. Turn round, hiss and scratch the fool hard on its silly, soft, wet nose.

Beware of hamsters. They taste good, but if you put your nose too near to their cage, they will bite you. And it hurts . . .

Cars are monsters that have slaughtered many cats. At night they dazzle and hypnotise you with their big eyes before smashing you to bits. Stay indoors at night.

Bubbles in the bath taste quite good and the water glitters in the light. But if you fall in, you will have to wash yourself three or four times to get rid of that revolting human smell.

Keep human intruders out of your home by climbing on the lap of guests who dislike cats. Follow them into the bathroom and sneer. Lick the butter on the table in front of them. Investigate and clean your private parts during conversation.

If human mating activities interfere with your sleep, take a firm line. Put an end to these interruptions by sleeping between the human pair. If necessary, rehome one of the humans.

Some humans mistakenly believe that babies are a substitute for cats. If your human decides on children as pets, rehome yourself.

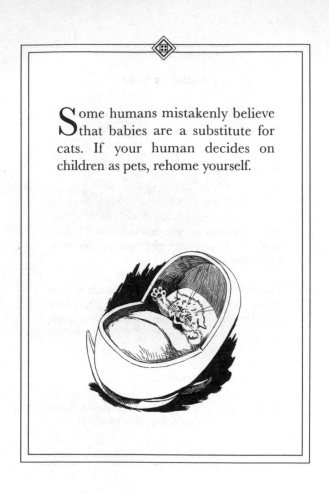

Author's Note

A proportion of the royalties of this book will go to Cats Protection, 17 Kings Road, Horsham, West Sussex RH13 5PN (helpline: 01403 221919; website: www.cats.org.uk). Please remember the plight of unwanted elderly cats who have ended up on the streets or found themselves homeless at the death of their owner. Elderly cats, disabled cats or cats with behaviour problems always need homes urgently. If you can give one (or more) a home, please do.

I want to thank the Newbury branch of Cats Protection for their help in Spring 2001. Like all CP branches, they need help with fundraising, home checking, fostering and all the other tasks of helping cats and kittens. If you live in their area and love cats, consider becoming a volunteer helper. Contact them at Cats Protection Newbury and District Branch, Heatherpine Shelter, Curridge Road, Curridge, Thatcham, Berkshire RG18 9DH.

Useful Information

For pet behaviour counsellors, contact the Association of Pet Behaviour Counsellors, PO Box 46, Worcester WR8 9YS (telephone: 01386 751151; website: www.apbc.org.uk). Alternatively, contact the Centre of Applied Pet Ethology, PO Box 6, Fortrose, Ross-shire IV10 8WB (website: www.coape.f9.co.uk).

A good place to start if you want feline information is the Feline Advisory Bureau, Taeselbury, High Street, Tisbury, Wiltshire SP3 6LD (telephone: 01747 871872; website: www.fabcats.org). FAB has useful leaflets on cat problems and cat diseases, all of which are available on its website or can be obtained by sending a large s.a.e. to them.